British Bro

John Kruse

May 2023

(cover illustration by Alice B Woodward from Juliana Horatia Ewing, *Brownies and Other Tales*, 1920)

Contents

Preface...5

Distribution 9

    Place...9

    Time...12

Brownie Nature 15

    Appearance 15

    Character..18

        Labouring Lobs 18

        Dim Dobbies 19

        Lazy Lobs...21

        Bad Brownies..21

    Dwellings 22

Domestic Functions...24

    Household Chores..25

    Farm Work...27

    Supervising Servants.....................................28

    Care for the Family 30

Other Powers 33

Payment..35

    Food- 'Wages' & Offerings 36

    Clothing & Laying 38

    Banishing the Brownie...................................41

Related Beings...44

Brownies in British Culture 49

Modern Brownies 55

Appendix 60

Preface

This book focusses upon the British brownie, the domestic spirit that chooses a particular house, or family, and will dutifully serve it across generations, undertaking household and farmyard chores, ostensibly for free. Needless to say, as a supernatural being, relations between brownies and humans are more complex than that and their good will is often forfeit, but the voluntary provision of labour is the basis of the interaction.

Before we go any further, it is necessary to pin down the subject of this essay more precisely. Brownies aren't by any means the only faery beings living in close association with humans, so we need to try to exclude the types that I won't cover here. The brownie (or broonie in Scotland) is a known class of supernatural, long recorded in folklore, and I shall very much respect the people who first conveyed these accounts to folklorists, and assume that they knew what they were talking about and chose their words with care and deliberation. The brownie can be thought of as relatively small and hairy. This seems to me to differentiate it from the larger and stronger hob, hobgoblin and lob. It also distinguishes the brownie from the boggart, another being that's found in human homes, but which has ghost-like as well as faery characteristics. Many faeries come into human homes- often to wash, to eat our food or to simply enjoy the warmth and facilities- and some (like Puck) will do the odd chore, but the brownie is distinct from those because of his almost permanent residence and single-minded dedication.

These categories, ultimately, are not hard and fast- witness Juliana Ewing in the introduction to her *Lob Lie by the Fire* of 1883, where she described her character as a "rough kind of brownie or house elf, supposed to haunt some north country homesteads, where he does the work of the farm labourer, for no grander wages than his 'cream bowl daily set' [quoting Milton]." Likewise, one modern folklore writer has observed that the creatures once termed boggarts in Yorkshire tend now to be classed as hobgoblins or brownies. The terminology is a lot looser now because we have so much less practical, personal experience of these beings- and many people (this author included) write not from their own knowledge but from book learning. For this reason too, therefore, I will prefer the terms used by contemporaries.[1]

In Highland Scotland we will encounter similar beings- the *gruagach, loireag* and *uruisg-* which can undertake certain farmwork but generally also have a separate life which involves more anti-social and even violent behaviours (as is also the case with many boggarts and some hobs). Some Scottish writers have termed these creatures brownies, but others have viewed them as more sinister and demonic, calling them *bodachs.* All of these are akin to brownies, but are treated by the local population as identifiably unique. I will therefore not cover them here- and what's more, I've already given these creatures extended treatment in my book *Beyond Faery.*[2]

Just like the English boggart, the Scottish broonie can shade into a ghost, and there are accounts in which spirits of the deceased perform brownie-like functions, such as undertaking household tasks and helping individuals in need of a midwife. The Cauld Lad of Hilton, in Northumberland, is another such anonymous being. He would work in the hall kitchen at night, tidying up what was left in a mess but throwing around and dirtying whatever had been tidied. Eventually, he was laid with the gift of a cloak and hood (see later) and disappeared forever. All of this is typical brownie behaviour, but the Cauld Lad was at least half-ghost, being believed to be the spirit of a stable boy killed in a rage by a former Lord of Hilton. The Dobie of Mortham in Teesdale was said to be the ghost of a

---

[1] K Roberts, *Folklore of Yorkshire,* 2013, 95; see too my *Beyond Faery,* 2020, c.9.
[2] MacGregor, *Peat Fire Flame,* 1937, c.4; Shaw, *History of the Province of Moray,* 1775, 306; see again my *Beyond Faery,* 2020, c.8.

woman murdered by a Lord of Rokeby and haunted an ancient tower. Her troubled spirit was eventually laid under a bridge.[3]

Lastly, we may note that brownies are generally "innominate," but the class may also be referred to collectively as Dobbs, Master Dobbs, Dobby and Dobie. There are also just a few named brownies, though as a rule, they are known only by reference to the farm or house to which they're attached. Amongst those who *are* named is Aiken Drum, the brownie of Blednoch in Galloway, who was driven away from the house when the owner's new wife gave him a pair of her husband's old trousers. Maggy Mulloch will be discussed later; whilst the being called Puddlefoot was banished by the very act of naming him. He lived in a burn between Pitlochry and Dunkeld in Perthshire and visited a nearby farm where he did some useful work but often caused more havoc than help. He tidied an untidy house, but would untidy a tidy house- as well as leaving wet footprints everywhere because his feet were always sodden from the burn. One night a drunken man passing heard the brownie splashing around as usual and addressed him as 'Puddlefoot.' Annoyed by the uncomplimentary soubriquet, he vanished forever.[4]

Brownies are, perhaps, not the most numerous of British faery creatures, but they are amongst the most attractive and memorable. People are aware of them who might never have heard of a boggart or a spriggan; this may be ascribed, I believe, to several factors: that they are closely associated with (and useful to) humans; that they are generally perceived as being benign and- possibly inseparable from the previous point- that their name evokes thoughts of furry domesticated

---

[3] J. Westwood & A. Kingshill, *The Lore of Scotland,* 2009, 310 & 316; *County Folklore,* vol.2, 'North Yorkshire, 95.

[4] L. Henderson & E. Cowan, *Scottish Fairy Belief,* 2004, 16; W. Nicholson, 'The Brownie of Blednoch;' Briggs, *Dictionary of Fairies,* 337; J. Westwood & A. Kingshill, *The Lore of Scotland,* 60.

animals. It's more complex than that, as of course- so here's
a field guide to the British brownie.

Distribution

Where are brownies to be encountered, both in space and time? Suffice to say, they are one of the oldest known and most widespread of the British faery beings.

Place

Brownies are, it might be said, a feature of the Anglo-Saxon part of Britain. They are known from East Anglia (Norfolk, Suffolk and Essex) up through Northern England (though mainly the North East, because in the North West the boggart performs many of the same roles) and they have colonised much of the Scottish lowlands, where they are called *broonies*.

Fascinatingly, the brownie is seldom found in the Gaelic speaking Highlands (or he's very hard to separate out from the *gruagach* and *loireag*- see the Preface) but he re-appears in the far north and west, on some of the Hebridean islands and in Orkney and Shetland, where he is called Broonie, King of the Trows. Here, he will take a particular farm and its corn fields under his care and can be glimpsed gliding from farm yard to farm yard, casting his protective spell over the growing crops. He does not like to be watched, though, and will scatter the hay ricks if he feels spied upon.   This wilful damage excepted, it was said on the islands that the brownies' stacks of corn would resist storms and never overturn, even though they were not bound with straw ropes or fenced, unlike normal human stacks.[5] On Orkney there is the additional tradition of the *hogboon,* or hill-dweller, another sort of trow who performs farm chores in return for food. New tenants of a farm at Helkhowe, on Sanday, weren't aware of the customary way of treating their *hogboon* and failed to give him his due share of ale, milk and cakes. As a result, he

---

[5] C. Rogers, *Social Life in Scotland,* 1886, vol.3, 249; M. Martin, *A Description of the Western Isle of Scotland,* 1716, 391; *County Folklore,* vol.3, 'Shetland & Orkney,' 21.

played many little tricks such as hiding items. They resolved to try to escape him by moving out, but he simply moved with them-a version of the 'flitting' story we shall encounter again.[6]

Cornwall, in the far southwest of Britain, presents us with a puzzling problem. There are some records of a brownie-like being there- and the term 'browney' is used- but the region is, at the same time, a long way from the nearest English brownie haunts, such as those of Mr Dobbs in Sussex, and is very far indeed from the regions where the term 'brownie' is widely used. Hence, as early (at least) as 1910, Walter Evans Wentz's informant on Cornish folklore, Henry Jenner, suggested that the term 'brownie' was most probably a foreign importation, "borrowed from books, though a 'brownie' *eo nomine* has been reported from Sennen within the last twenty years."[7]

The conviction that there was a Cornish 'browney' derives from Robert Hunt's *Popular Romances of the West of England* (1865) in which he identified five types of faery being in Cornwall. He went on to describe his 'browney' class as being a spirit:

> "purely of the household. Kindly and good, he devoted his every care to benefit the family with whom he had taken up his abode. The Browney has fled, owing to his being brought into very close contact with the schoolmaster, and he is only summoned now upon the occasion of the swarming of the bees. When this occurs, mistress or maid seizes a bell-metal, or a tin pan, and, beating it, she
> calls 'Browney, Browney!' as loud as she can until the good Browney compels the bees to settle."[8]

---

[6] E. Marwick, *The Folklore of Orkney & Shetland,* 1975, 41.
[7] Evans Wentz, *The Fairy Faith in Celtic Countries,* 1911, 165.
[8] Hunt, *Popular Romances of the West of England,* 5 & 82.

Hunt's Browney is the typical English and Scots brownie, but with a special interest in apiculture (which *is* a feature of the broonies of Galloway, in south west Scotland). This paragraph is also virtually the only mention of him in Cornwall. Nevertheless, fifteen years- in 1881- a Mr. Cornish, the town clerk of Penzance, informed an antiquarian meeting held in the town "that there was a brownie still existing [there]; that a gentleman, whose opinion he would take on many matters, had told him that he had often seen it sitting quietly by the fireside." We can only assume that this being did some domestic chores as well; I also wonder whether Henry Jenner's Sennen brownie was a faulty recall of the Penzance case.[9]

Nonetheless, what is known in Cornwall is what may be called a truly domesticated pixie, acting to all intents and purposes exactly like a northern English brownie- and attached to a particular family or house. These beings happily undertake a range of household chores and cleaning, just so long as they are not watched by the occupants. One is recorded to have appeared over a period of months in a farmhouse kitchen at Werrington, near Launceston, taking the form of a small child. It was treated very much as a member of the household, being given its own stool to sit upon by the fire, and it did a great deal of housework. If the chimney and hearth had not been swept, it would pinch the maid. Another 'house pixie' was to be found at Killigarth manor, near Polperro. There, it supervised the cooking in the kitchen, watching the roast on the spit over the fire and getting a servant to remove the meat when it was cooked.[10]

---

[9] R. Cromek, *Remains of Nithsdale & Galloway Song,* 337; M. Courtney, *Cornish Feasts & Folklore,* 1890, 123; *The Cornishman,* November 17th 1881, 7, 'Natural History and Antiquarian Society;' S. Young, 'Three Cornish Fairy Notes,' *Devon & Cornwall Notes & Queries,* 41, 2012, 2.
[10] *Notes & Queries,* 1st series, vol.2 (1850), 475; Couch, 'Cornish Folklore,' *Penzance Natural History & Antiquarian Society Report,* in *Royal Cornwall Gazette,* Nov.11th, 1853, 7.

Most notably, an old Cornish mill had a pixie attached to it, who used to do the grinding for customers. As well as his manual labours, he had a keen moral sense. He always gave full measure to people, unlike the miller himself, and the pixie would often tickle the miller's palm to remind him he was cheating. One day, there was an error in a delivery and an argument developed between the miller and his wife. To begin with the husband blamed her, but then the man started blaming the pixie. For this wrongful accusation, the pixie swore not to do another stroke of work in the mill for the next two generations: this adverse reaction to criticism is a known brownie trait elsewhere in Britain, as we shall discover.[11]

'Domestic pixies' therefore seem to have been known in Cornwall, performing most of the functions of the brownie without the physical resemblances. Meanwhile, Robert Hunt's Browney- as faery authority Simon Young has argued- seems to be a fabrication, arising from a confused memory of some sources but not based upon any authentic Cornish usage. There appears never to have been a spirit that responded to the 'tanging' when bees swarmed.[12]

Time

The first mentions of brownies date from the late fifteenth and early sixteenth centuries and are exclusively Scottish. The poet, Sir John Rowll, in a verse called *Cursing,* mentioned the "Browny," as did the historian John Mair or Major, who described a spirit haunting his native North Berwick:

> "Those Fauns and those called *brobne* [brownies] are at home among us but do no harm… [they do such things] as to thresh out so much wheat in one night as twenty men could manage in that time [and] they throw pebbles

---

[11] Harris, *Cornish Saints and Sinners,* c.19; see too my *British Pixies,* Green Magic, 2021.
[12] S. Young, 'Against Taxonomy: The Fairy Families of Cornwall,' *Cornish Studies,* vol.21, 2013.

among those sitting near the fire in the country, seeming to laugh… Moreover, it is doubtful whether they can foretell the future… [But] there are some [spirits] among us Britons who foretell the future in prophetic fashion- about the death and murder of some." [13]

The Scottish poet Gavin (or Gawain) Douglas, published a translation of Virgil's *Aeneid* in 1513 in the preface to which he promised that: "Of Brownyis and of Bogillis full is this Buke." William Dunbar (1460-1520) composed *The Dance of the Seven Deadly Sins* in 1515; he mentioned two spirits, Black Belly and Bawsy Brown, the second of whom is thought to be a brownie: the meaning of the first element of his name means 'big' or 'clumsy,' which could be apt. A third Scot, Alexander Montgomery, published his verse, *The Flyting of Polwart,* in the early 1580s, and he too mentions the beings alongside other alarming spirits: "bogles, brownies, gyre carlings and ghaists."

Lastly, in 1597 King James IV of Scotland published his book *Daemonologie,* in which he gave some consideration to *pharies* and other supernatural beings. Amongst these was one "called Brownie in our language" who:

> "appeared in time of Papistrie and blindnesse, and haunted divers houses, without doing any evill, but doing as it were necessarie turnes up and down the house: and… who appeared like a rough-man: yea, some were so blinded, as to beleeve that their house was all the sonsier [fortunate or prosperous], as they called it, that such spirites resorted there."[14]

As we shall see in due course, the idea that the sheer presence of a brownie (over and above the work he performed) brought good luck to a holding was widespread

---

[13] *The Cursing of Sr. Johne Rowlis, Upoun the Steilaris of His Fowlis*, line 101; Mair, *Expositio in Matthaeum*, 1518, folio 48.
[14] James Stewart, *Daemonologie,* 1597, Book 3, c.3.

and longstanding: on leaving Bodsbeck for Liethin Hall, the brownie of the former declared "A' the luck of Bodsbeck's awa' to Liethinha'.". It can therefore easily be imagined how disastrous it could be if the brownie not only departed but, at the same time, cursed his former abode- as happened at Claypotts Castle near Dundee. The departing broonie pronounced his spell upon the castle and all its surrounding areas- which included "the thin sowens o' Drumgeith," indicative of a poor, starved place, and concluding:

> "[to] Clay-pats I'll gie my malison
> Come I late or come I air,
> Ballemie's board's aye bare..."[15]

Ballemie was a gentleman's house near to the castle, the bare tables of which once again imply a departed prosperity.

---

[15] R. Cromek, *Remains of Nithsdale & Galloway Song,* 333; R. Chambers, *Popular Rhymes,* 326.

Brownie Nature

The looks and temperament of the brownie are very consistent across the whole range of his presence in Britain.

Appearance

There is, by and large, a fairly settled view of the brownie's physical form. Perhaps the earliest report comes from Dyce near Aberdeen in 1601. One Walter Ronaldson was visited by a being "lyke ane litell bodie, haiffing scheavin berd, quhyt lening lyk an sark" ('like a small person, with a shaven beard [and[clad in white linen like a shirt'). Early folklore writer John Graham Dalyell regarded this small, hairy apparition as a brownie.[16]

In 1828, Irish antiquary Thomas Crofton Croker declared the brownie to be an elf- not very slim but well-proportioned and agreeable; Samuel Johnson called him a "sturdy fairy." Another early commentator equated the Scottish brownie with the English Robin Goodfellow, but agreed with Crofton Croker that he was "stout and blooming." Then again, he's been called "meagre, shaggy and wild in appearance." Highland author William Grant Stewart depicted the brownie both as a sort of "mongrel fairy" as well as being "not as tall as a fairy, but well-proportioned and comely." In Grant Stewart's view, what marked the being out was his brown complexion, which gave rise to the name (rather than, as most others seem to imply, his distinctively shaggy hair).[17]

---

[16] Dalyell, *The Darker Superstitions of Scotland,* 1834, 530; *Selections from the Records of Kirk Sessions, Presbytery & Synod of Aberdeen,* Spalding Club, 1846, 184.

[17] Crofton Croker, *Faery Legends & Traditions,* 1828, vol.3, 48; Johnson, *A Journey to the Western Isles,* 1774; T. Pennant, *A Tour of Scotland & a Voyage to the Hebrides,* 1772, 359; G. Brisbane Douglas, *Scottish Fairy & Folk Tales,* 1900, 177; Grant Stewart, *Popular Superstitions,* 139; *County Folklore,* vol.2, 'North Yorkshire,' 131- Whitbywash.

Far more authorities tended to agree with the Scottish author Robert Chambers that the brownie is "a spirit of somewhat grotesque figure, dwarfish in stature but endowed with great personal strength." So, for instance, demonologist George Sinclair in 1685 described the brownie as a helpful spirit that haunted divers houses, whose appearance was like that of "a rough, hairy man." The engraver Robert Cromek gave a description in 1810 which confirmed and expanded upon this. The Gallovidian brownie he was familiar with was "small of stature, covered with short curly hair, with brown matted locks and a brown mantle reaching to the knee and a hood of the same colour." One eighteenth century source described the species as "a' rough but the mouth" and another example was said to have been a "big, hairy man and entirely naked." Constance Gordon Cumming added some valuable details to this image: the brownie is dwarfish but extremely strong she, she confirmed, and he breathes heavily and has very large eyes. Furthermore, the species are long-lived, serving a family for several centuries; the brownie of Bodsbeck is known to have been with the family there for three hundred years before they unwisely drove him away.[18]

The 'shepherd poet' James Hogg in 1818 retold the story of the *Brownie of Bodsbeck*, in which a local man disguises himself as the titular brownie, thereby giving us an insight into popular conceptions of the spirit. Hogg's being is "a wee bit hurklin crile of an unearthly thing, shrinkit and as wan as he had lien seven years i' the grave… Its beard was long and grey, while its look and every lineament of its face was indicative of agony- its locks were thin, dishevelled and white and its back hunched up behind its head." The brownie was, therefore, a dwarf-like or deformed being which sat huddled up and looked emaciated and pale. Elsewhere, Hogg

---

[18] R. Chambers, *Popular Rhymes of Scotland,* 325; G. Sinclair, *Satan's Invisible World,* 1685, 214; R. Cromek, *Remains of Nithsdale & Galloway Song,* 1810, 330 & 332; MacRitchie, *Testimony of Tradition,* 160; *Legends of Scottish Superstition,* 1848, 28-30; C. Gordon Cumming, *In the Hebrides,* 1883, 173; Sir Walter Scott's Red Gauntlet was thick, short, shaggy and as hirsute as a lion.

overall character. Nonetheless, however devoted the brownie was to humans' best interests, he could play as many pranks and be as much a nuisance as a faery if he felt displeased or scorned.[23]

Dim Dobbies

Brownies may be strong and diligent, but they don't necessarily have the brains to match the brawn. The Mortham Dobie of County Durham was described as a "mortal heavy spirit" who was rather slow and dim. Hence typical sayings in the north that a not very bright person is "but a dobie" or a "stupid dobie."[24]

In fact, the very name of many northern brownies is a clue to their nature. 'Dobby' (and its variants) arose from 'Old Hob,' a familiar term for a devil or goblin in which the 'Hob' element was an abbreviation of Robert. The name evolved through 'Ol' Dob' to its current form and acquired a range of meanings, foremost amongst which was the sense of a person notable for some distinctive physical or mental attribute, especially an individual who is awkward, clumsy- or stupid. This plainly would apply to the large, strong brownie who was not agile of either mind or body. By way of comparison, consider the name 'dobbin,' often applied to large, plodding carthorses. It derives from Robin (as in the domestic hobgoblin Robin Goodfellow) and is, again, evocative of heaviness and sloth.[25]

At Tullochgorm in Strathspey there lived another brownie who wasn't so bright and who was known tellingly as Brownie Clod.

---

[23] *County Folklore,* vol.7, 'Clackmannanshire,' 317; J. Westwood & S. Kingshill, *The Lore of Scotland,* 2009, 56; Sir John Stoddard, *Remarks on the Local Scenery & Manners of Scotland During the Years 1799 & 1800,* 64; Sir Walter Scott, *Minstrelsy of the Scottish Borders,* vol.1, 54.
[24] W. Brockie, *Legends & Superstitions of the County of Durham,* 1886, 44.
[25] Scott, 'The Devil & His Imps,' *Transactions of the American Philological Association,* vol. 26, 1895, 79-89.

He was described as looking like a "young lad" and was a humorous prankster, whose idea of a great joke was throwing sods of earth at passers-by, but he was also rather simple, in one case being tricked into doing two men's work all winter in return for nothing more than an old coat and cowl. The Clod's sister, or wife, was a being resembling a "young lass" and was called Meg Moulach. A related creature, Maggy Moloch, was associated with Fincastle Mill in Perthshire. Her son was another rather dim being, called the Brownie of the Mill, who one night found a young girl grinding the flour for her wedding cake there (everyone else had refused to do it, precisely because of the mill's haunted reputation). The brownie sidled up to her and wanted to know her name, but she was canny enough to only disclose "*mise mi fein*" (me myself). Brownie kept on making unwelcome advances, so she threw scalding water over him. His screams attracted Maggy, who wanted to know the culprit, but all he could say before he died was "Me myself."[26]

To conclude, a tale is also told of a Galloway brownie who spent the entire night rounding up a herd of sheep. Afterwards he complained about the difficulties he'd faced with some of the flock: "Deil tak' thae wee grey beasties- they cost me mair fash than a' the lave of them" ('The devil take the little grey ones- they cost me more effort than all the rest'). An inspection of the fold revealed that he'd also gathered in half a dozen hares- hence his bother. An identical story is found on the Isle of Man, this time describing the hob-like *fynoderee*; in both cases, the point is to underline the dogged determination of the being- unmatched, however, by brains or common sense.[27]

---

[26] Grant Stewart, *Popular Superstitions,* 142; W. Forsyth, *In the Shadow of Cairngorm,* 1900, c.4; Briggs, *Dictionary of Fairies,* 48; Westwood & Kingshill, *The Lore of Scotland,* 78-79.

[27] J. Maxwell Wood, *Witchcraft & Superstitious Record in the South Western District of Scotland,* 191; see my *Manx Fairies,* 2022; Katherine Briggs also mentions such an incident from Lancashire: *The Fairies in Tradition & Literature,* 1968, 31.

In contradiction of all that has been said so far, there is a body of opinion that the brownie is, innately, idle. Whilst a sense of duty might provoke incredible exertions- when necessary, the creature's preference is to enjoy basking in the warmth of the hearth, stretched out at leisure (albeit becoming noisy and disruptive as the embers cool over the course of a night). Thus, the dobie at Mortham Tower, near Barnard Castl,e would perform chores like a brownie in times of need- but her tendency was naturally to be lazy.[28]

Bad Brownies

The aforementioned Mortham dobie also had a violent streak, which meant that she would occasionally jump up behind horse riders and squeeze them to death. This discloses to us the other, little acknowledged, aspect of brownies- the fact that some can be positively dangerous to humans.[29]

Several writers have drawn a distinction between the helpful brownies who live in close proximity to people and those that inhabit lonely barns and granges, ruined towers and old bridges, far away from humankind. These "more gloomy dobbies" are "full of mischievous and malignant tricks and play pranks on benighted travellers." These practical 'jokes' tend to be jumping up behind lone riders and fatally hugging them; the victims will then either quickly die before they reach their destinations or will fall into "some dreadful and lingering malady."[30]

---

[28] R. Willan, 'A List of Ancient Words At Present Used in the Mountainous District of the West Riding of Yorkshire,' *Archaeologia,* vol.17, 1814, 138-167; W. Henderson, *Folklore of the Northern Counties,* 247; Sternberg, *The Dialect & Folklore of Northamptonshire,* 1851, 193.
[29] W. Henderson, *Folklore of the Northern Counties,* 247.
[30] Washington Irving, *Bracebridge Hall,* 1822, vol.2, 56-58; Willan, 'A List of Ancient Words,' *Archaeologia,* vol.17, 1814, 138-167

Not every home should expect to have a brownie. According to Robert Cromek, they only associate with families who are "eminent for their ancestry and virtue." Grant Stewart therefore called the brownie "the heirloom of an ancient and honourable family." They will, accordingly, live in those families' castles and mansions. Other writers have been more liberal, alleging instead that "almost every family" in Scotland had its attendant sprite. Another, perhaps better, opinion was that a brownie would serve any good and worthy family, but would also help out the unfortunate poor as well.[31]

Some brownies are said to live in the cellars or dungeons of the houses they serve or, at least, to hide somewhere about the property, such as in the outhouses, byres and barns, as was the case on a farm at Ulzieside in Upper Nithsdale.[32] Even so, whilst there is an understandable tendency to assume that all brownies live in the houses or farms to which they're attached, this is not always the case. They are, by nature, solitary beings, and in south west Scotland we know them to frequent hollow trees, or to stay in old castles even after the family has moved out and the structures have fallen into ruin. Nonetheless, these hiding places will always be near to the property to which they're attached, yet sufficiently separated to allow a little privacy and peace during daytime. In these places the brownie is "unseen and idle" during the day, resting and recuperating before his nocturnal exertions commence again.[33]

---

[31] Cromek, *Remains of Nithsdale & Galloway Song,* 330; Grant Stewart, *Popular Superstitions,* 141; *Legends of Scottish Superstition,* 1848, 'Maclachlan's Brownie;' J. Maxwell Wood, *Witchcraft & Superstitious Record in the South Western District of Scotland,* 1911, 187.
[32] *Legends of Scottish Superstition,* 'Maclachlan's Brownie;' J. F. Campbell, *West Highland Tales,* vol.1, xlvii; Wilson, *Folklore of Uppermost Nithsdale,* 63.
[33] Cromek, *Remains of Nithsdale & Galloway Song,* 330; Chambers, *Popular Rhymes,* 325.

Living remotely from the premises to which he's attached also created a situation which proved the dedication of the brownie of Cash in Strathmiglo parish, Fife. Finding his normal ford across a burn impassable because the waters had risen, he uncomplainingly made a long detour to use a bridge so that he could get to the house to do his work.[34]

---

[34] H. Aitken, *A Forgotten Heritage*, 1973, 37; D. MacRitchie, *Hints of Evolution in Tradition*, 7.

"Then the brownie, he's a kind o' half-spirit half-man; he'll drudge an' do a' the wark about the town for his meat, but then he'll no work but when he likes- for a' the king's dominions."[35]

In most cases, the brownie worked hard- and for free- around homes and agricultural holdings. In Sussex the association between the local brownie, Dobbs, and huge quantities of work, was preserved in the saying "Master Dobbs has been helping you," indicating an individual who's overwhelmed by their workload.[36]

As Robert Cromek stated, brownies are "somewhat coy in their manner of work." That residing at Bodsbeck Hall in Dumfriesshire only ever showed itself once to the new laird when he had inherited the property and, most of the time, all that anyone ever saw of him was a fleeting glimpse of a hand. This secrecy was, of course, compounded by brownies' preference for working at night when all the human household were out of the way in bed.[37]

Sometimes, the brownie was more of a domestic guardian spirit than a household servant, as was the case with the Kendal Dobbie. He lived by the fireside and tended to be rather over-familiar with the family whose home he shared. They decided to move to escape his presence, giving rise to a typical 'flitting' story. The night before the planned removal, the dobbie was seen in the byre and was asked what he was doing, to which he replied "Oh, nowt- nobbut greasin' mi shoon: we're gaan to skift to-morn" (Oh, nothing but polishing my shoes- we're going to move house tomorrow". They family

---

[35] James Hogg, *The Woolgatherer*, 1818.
[36] Wright, *Rustic Speech & Folklore*, 1913, 202.
[37] Cromek, *Remains of Nithsdale & Galloway Song*, 330.

decided to stay after all, given the futility of trying to leave their dobbie behind.[38]

Given the range of chores he undertook, people had to comply the conditions he imposed. They had to respect his privacy and they had to put up with his practical jokes. The brownie's pranks were just something to be tolerated by the household- an unavoidable element of faery makeup. Just like other faery beings, the brownie could become invisible, so that a story is told of one who sat himself between two maidservants who were furtively sharing a bowl of brose (a thick kind of porridge made with oatmeal) that their niggardly employer would not have allowed them. The brownie swallowed a mouthful of their meal every time that the spoon was passed between them, so that he ate twice as much as either of the girls- and laughed at their disappointment afterwards. In Herefordshire the brownie was known as a decidedly domestic being, who'd sit on the 'crook' or 'sway' (from which pots were hung) over the fire. If he was slighted, he would take revenge by hiding the household keys. The only way to recover them then would be to put a small cake on the hob and for everyone to sit patiently around the hearth, with their eyes closed and in silence. The brownie would in due course relent and would return the keys by throwing them against the wall.[39]

Household Chores

The brownie was a "mysterious and very useful agent" in a house; as Robert Cromek put it, "in family economy, they were unrivalled." The domestic brownies would undertake the full range of household chores overnight, whilst family and servants slept. They would perform all the menial tasks of the lowly servants, washing the dishes and dairy implements like the churn, sweeping and washing the floors, gathering

---

[38] B. Kirkby, *Lakeland Words,* 1898, 76-77.
[39] R. Cromek, *Remains of Nithsdale & Galloway Song,* 336; E. Leather, *Folklore of Herefordshire,* 1912, 47.

25

firewood, bringing in water from the well or spring and undertaking demanding and laborious tasks such as keeping the dairy thoroughly clean.[40]

Over and above daily chores, brownies looked after the bees in the hives and helped make the butter come in the churns. In Sussex, it has been proposed that a rhyme used to protect dairies from witches might also have been used to invoke the aid of 'Dobbs' to get the butter to come if it was proving slow. The little doggerel charm goes as follows:

"Come, butter, come,
Come, butter, come,
Peter stands at the gate,
Waiting for a buttered cake,
Come butter, come."

Repeating Dobbs' name three times is reported to have had the same effect- and may have in fact been confused with the witch charm.[41]

The brownie at Castle Lachlan on Loch Fyne is even more attentive to the needs of inhabitants. It's said that he will tour the rooms of the castle at night, making sure that the bedding covers the sleepers. On the island of Gigha, the Cara brownie lived in the ancient mansion of the MacDonalds and would make all the preparations for guests visiting (as well as slapping them if they disrespected the castle). These tasks included tidying up, readying the beds and putting the dogs in the kennels (or, apparently, killing them if they were left inside).[42]

---

[40] Grant Stewart, *Popular Superstitions,* 139; R. Cromek, *Remains of Nithsdale & Galloway Song,* 338; *Old Statistical Accounts,* vol.9, 1793, 328- Tongland, Kirkcaldy.

[41] R. Cromek, *Remains of Nithsdale & Galloway Song,* 337; J. Simpson, 'Fairy Queens & Pharisees,' chapter 1 in Young & Houlbrook, *Magical Folk,* 2018, 30; C. Latham, 'Some West Sussex Superstitions Lingering in 1868,' *Folk-Lore Record,* vol.1, 1878, 28; J. Simpson, *Folklore of Sussex,* 1973, 57.

Around the Ochil Hills of Perthshire, stories were told of the local brownies and especially of one called Tod Lowrie or Red Bonnet. A little girl who lived with her grandmother hoped to see him or one of the faeries, as many children would, but this came about in an unexpected way. The grandmother fell ill and the child struggled to run the household. That night, though, the brownie came and undertook many of the chores- sweeping the floors, washing the dishes, bringing in fresh water and making porridge for breakfast. Whilst he was at work, it snowed heavily, and he was unable to open the door to leave, so he tried to go up the chimney. The soot made him sneeze, which woke the little girl, who glimpsed her secret helper before he vanished.[43]

Farm Work

Around any farm or small holding, in the barns and in mills, the brownie would perform a wide range of time consuming or laborious tasks. Out in the fields, he would carry food for the livestock, plant, weed, reap and bring in the grain, mow and cock the hay, collect horses from the pastures and saddle them, guard the corn stacks, he would raddle, lamb and shear the sheep, mend fences and hedges and dig ditches. Around the farm buildings, he would store and thresh as much harvested grain as ten men, winnowing, sifting and sacking it up with great care so that none was lost; he would finely grind the stored corn and ensure that the hens didn't lay away from their roosts. Most astonishing of all would be the brownie's energy and workmanship: although he performed alone the work of many farm labourers, he did not tire and would maintain throughout the highest standards.[44]

---

[42] A. MacGregor, *Peat Fire Flame,* 1937, 47 & 48.
[43] R. Menzies Fergusson, *Ochil Fairy Tales,* 1912, 8.
[44] Dalyell, *Darker Superstitions,* 530; R. Cromek, *Remains of Nithsdale & Galloway Song,* 330-333; W. Thornber, *Historical & Descriptive Account of Blackpool,* 1837, 332.

An interesting variant upon the theme of the brownie's care for the farm is the story of the brownie of Butterdean Wood in East Lothian. The son of the farmer was found to be abusing one of the ponies in the farm's livestock, so the brownie saved it and then abandoned the estate, taking the pony with him into the wood.[45]

Some brownies could take their devotion too far, though, going so far as to steal produce from neighbouring farms in order to supply their master or mistress. In one Scottish case, he made himself straw leggings which he filled up with the milk from another's cows.[46]

It's alleged that, at Cleiton near Pitlochry, there used to be a mill that was worked by some brownies. If you left a sack of corn there overnight, it would be ground by the morning, with a reasonable sum taken as a fee for the milling. This is a unique instance of the brownie setting up business alone and for himself. Nevertheless, it may have been observed how often mills have so far been mentioned in connection with brownies; in fact, they seem to have a broader fascination for faery kind, being places they like to frequent at night, more often for leisure than for labour. The brownie, like many other faeries, likes to eat bread, so grinding flour may be part of the attraction. Perhaps the high likelihood of humans *not* being in mills at night was a more compelling reason for faeries to assemble in them so that they could meet and dance undisturbed.[47]

Supervising Servants

---

[45] T. Porteus, *East Lothian Folk Tales,* 2017, c.10.
[46] *Tobar an dulchais,* November 1978.
[47] J Dixon, *Pitlochry- Past & Present,* 1925, 133; see my *Faery,* 2020, c.8 on faery food and *How Things Work in Faery,* Green Magic, 2021, 80, 'Faeries in the Corn Fields' for details of their arable production and processing.

The brownie will stand in for the master in supervising servants- and will punish those he considers to be lazy or dishonest. Rather less creditably, perhaps, the brownie might also spy on the serving staff and then report on their conduct to their master and mistress. Plainly, this made him no friends in the serving hall, so that one folklorist had to remark upon the importance of a householder ensuring that his staff continued to care for the brownie, leaving out food and drink, despite his snitching, so as to avoid further antagonising him.[48]

The most famous of these brownie-overseers was Mag Mhullach or Hairy Meg of Tullochgorm in Strathspey. She served the Grant family, being an honest and excellent housekeeper who paid very close attention to cleanliness and order. Most memorably, she could lay the table by using magic- conveying whatever dishes were asked for through the air to the diners, but she also spied on, and told stories about, the staff, who in revenge mocked her for her hairy left hand.[49]

The MacNeills of Cariskey had a brownie who, when other gentry came to visit the family, would pull the maids out of their beds at night and make them clean the house if their preparations weren't considered to have been adequate. The Cara brownie of the MacDonalds would hit untidy or lazy servants in dark corners of the house, or would play unkind tricks upon them- so, for example, one man was taken out of his bed and left naked in front of the kitchen fire to be discovered by everyone the next morning. In some houses, animosity arose with the domestic staff simply because of the brownie's look and habits. One, a large, hairy, naked being, used to enter the house nightly by the chimney, severely scaring the house-maids. One night, one of the women heated up the crook used for hanging pots over the hearth, so that the brownie was badly burned as he tried to get in. He

---

[48] G. Brisbane Douglas, *Scottish Fairy & Folk Tales,* 177; Grant Stewart, *Popular Superstitions,* 141.
[49] Grant Stewart, *Popular Superstitions,* 143.

took his revenge the next day by holding her face down on the hot baking stone.[50]

There wasn't always hostility between domestic staff and brownies, though. The Perthshire being called Maggy Molloch was hired to work by some farm servants who gave her bread and cream in return. When the farmer himself found out about the arrangement, he determined to get rid of his human employees and just retain the much cheaper and more energetic brownie. Maggy went on strike and became a nuisance around the farm until he relented.[51]

Care for the Family

Inside the house, as well as housekeeping duties, the brownie's tasks included such 'maternal' or traditionally female activities as child care and rocking the cradle. In one Gaelic story, the family's brownie is said to have delivered the baby whilst the husband was absent, still fetching the midwife. In another, the spirit saved a pregnant women from her mother-in-law's witchcraft. The husband's mother disliked his young wife and used spells to delay her delivery, but fortunately the brownie detected the magic and counteracted it.[52]

The brownie would protect both the honour, and the person, of the women of a house. So, for example, the brownie of the Maxwells of Dalswinton not only undertook his farmwork but escorted the family's daughter to trysts with her sweethearts, prepared her for her wedding night by removing her clothes before she got into bed with her new husband and fetched the midwife when she was confined.[53]

---

[50] Westwood & Kingshill, *The Lore of Scotland,* 9; MacGregor, *Peat Fire Flame,* 48; *Legends of Scottish Superstition*, 1848, 28-30.
[51] Briggs, *Dictionary of Fairies,* 1977, 48-49.
[52] Dalyell, *Darker Superstitions,* 530; *Tobar an dulchais,* December 11th 1976 & April 28th 1988.
[53] R. Cromek, *Remains of Nithsdale & Galloway Song,* 333; Westwood & Kingshill, *The Lore of Scotland,* 140-141.

The brownie's care for the family (as well, indeed, for the servants of the household) extended to their moral welfare. He would listen in to any fireside chatter and gossip and would intervene whenever he was concerned that unworthy intentions were being expressed, most especially in matters of love.[54]

The aforementioned Mag Mhullach in Tullochmore also made herself responsible for ensuring that the laird got home safely at night if he had been out drinking. The brownie of Noltland Castle, on the island of Westray in the Orkneys, not only performed conventional functions, such as constructing and repairing bridges, and hauling boats above the high-water mark during storms, but he fetched a doctor for the lady of the castle when she was ill.[55]

Curiously, though, there is a record from Shetland of a charm against supernatural harm, recited to protect children from taking by the brownie:

"Hushaba minner's dattie,
We shall put the trows awa'
Broonie sanna get the bairn,
And if he comes the cocks'll craa."[56]

Perhaps this spell is echoed in a statement from the Lake District that indicates that the brownie might keep the children of a household on their best behaviour, just as he did with servants, fulfilling a role much akin to bugbears and other 'nursery sprites.' An old man told folklorist Henry Cowper how, when he had been a boy "dobbies and sic like were aw

---

[54] J. Maxwell Wood, *Witchcraft & Superstitious Record in the South Western District of Scotland,* 187
[55] MacGregor, *Peat Fire Flame,* 54; Westwood & Kingshill, *The Lore of Scotland,* 397.
[56] *Tobar an dulchais,* August 8th 1961.

up and down and t' childer hardly dare put their noses ayont t' threshold at neet."[57]

The attachment to a family or clan could run much deeper than simple care giving. The Killichoan brownie was very attached to the Maclachlans and would cry and wail at a waterfall near their home if one was heading off to war. One time, the being told a servant not to miss out any element of a final meal before a young Maclachlan headed off to battle; the salt was forgotten, nonetheless, and the young man died, suggesting that the brownie also had some control over fate as well.

The brownie attached to MacNeill's of Cariskey was similar. When Colonel MacNeill went off to fight, the brownie accompanied him, sitting on his horse's saddle in front of his body to protect him from bullets. On one occasion, the colonel tried to stop the brownie and she slapped him for his foolish presumption.   A very similar account is given of the 'Little One,' the brownie of the MacKays of Kintrye, who went with his master to the Peninsula war. The female gender of the MacNeill spirit is notable, and may indicate some cross-over into the idea of the banshee (*bean sith*) in these cases.[58]

---

[57] H. S. Cowper, *Hawkshead,* 1899, 308.
[58] Lord Archibald Campbell, *Records of Argyll,* 1885, 187 & 375; MacGregor, *Peat Fire Flame,* 49.

Other Powers

Besides an aptitude for unstinting physical labour, brownies have many other skills, such as being skilled players of backgammon, as in the case of the MacLeods of Berneray on Harris, or chess, as was the case with the aforementioned Mag Mhullach. More importantly, they have a range of magical powers over and above their huge capacity for hard work over a short time. For example, they can grant wishes for their humans: the brownie called Meg Mholach at Achnarrow, in Glenlivet, would answer her household's wish for more produce by making more cheeses; another supplied a magic bottle which provided the owner with an endless supply of money.[59]

Some domestic brownies have been entrusted to guard the family gold and silver (especially when it's been buried). At Craufurdland, near Kilmarnock, a brownie guarded a pot of gold buried beneath a pool beneath a bridge. The local laird there wanted to try to recover the treasure, and dammed and drained the pool to do so; just as he seemed to be on the point of finding the hoard, the brownie called out that the laird's tower was on fire. The work was abandoned promptly and, by the time it was realised that this was a false alarm and the laird returned to the river, his work had been undone and the pool was full again. It's just a short step from these ideas to the case of the dobbie of Crosby Hall at Crosby Ravensworth in the Lake District, who had the common faery ability to detect buried treasure. He left the Hall after the old pele tower he had inhabited was demolished, but not before telling the resident farmer where a hidden hoard was concealed- and, probably rather less welcome information, when and how the man would die.[60]

---

[59] MacGregor, *Peat Fire Flame,* 50; Westwood & Kingshill, *The Lore of Scotland,* 460-461; *Tobar an dulchais,* Feb. 16th 1979 & 1956; J. McPherson, *Primitive beliefs in the North East of Scotland,* 1929, 107.
[60] R. Chambers, *Popular Rhymes,* 241-242; Westwood & Kingshill, *The Lore of Scotland,* 177; J. Sullivan, *Cumberland & Westmorland- Ancient &*

As well as having access to secret information, then, brownies also enjoy powers of prophecy. Meg Mollach was also able to foretell deaths, for example, and a brownie appeared to the Campbell lord of Kilchurn Castle in Argyll to warn him of impending trouble at home, enabling him to return quickly to deal with it.[61]

Lastly, the brownies' powers of prophecy could manifest themselves in behaviour akin to the banshee. The brownie of Goranberry Tower, Roxburghshire, who was called the 'Cowie,' was a typical being in that he got in peats for the fire, raddled the sheep, cut firewood, spun wool and ground meal in the quern. In addition, though, if he lamented, it was a sure sign that there would be a death in the family.[62]

Modern, 1857, 136.
[61] Grant Stewart, *Popular Superstitions,* 141; R. Sim, *Legends of Strathisla,* 1848, 7; Westwood & Kingshill, *The Lore of Scotland,* 29-30.
[62] C. Rogers, *Social Life in Scotland,* 1886, vol.3, 248.

Payment

The brownie should never be directly or blatantly 'paid' or rewarded for its labours. Recompense can be provided, but it has to be done subtly and discretely, and should never include actual money.[63]

Even a word of thanks or praise can drive a brownie off- as, for that matter, can any hint of criticism or mockery. Hence, when two brownies helped a smith at Glamis he congratulated them the next morning- and they both instantly vanished. Equally, when the garnering and thrashing of corn undertaken in the barn by the spirit at Cranshaws Farm in Berwickshire was not fully appreciated, the whole crop was thrown off a crag two miles distant. As is often the case, the brownie used verse to express his fury at the slighting of his 'mowing' (in the sense of piling in the barn):

> "It's no weel mow'd! It's no weel mow'd!
> Then it's ne'er be mowed by me again,
> I'll scatter it owre the Raven Stane
> And they'll hae some wark ere it's mowed again."

As well as losing his labour in the future, the farm labourers had- effectively- to harvest their grain all over again- and with far more effort expended. Even worse misfortunes occurred at Rothiemurchus, where the Grant family's brownie used to clean the house at night; one night the loud clatter of pots and pans in the kitchen woke the laird, who complained volubly at the racket, and the brownie was gone the next morning. At Invergarry, the brownie deserted the house after one of the servants scolded him. He had embodied the good fortune of the property, so that for some time after he departed, all the domestic affairs went wrong. This does imply, though, that matters may eventually recover, even if the brownie never returns.[64]

---

[63] Sir Walter Scott, *Minstrelsy of the Scottish Borders,* vol.1, 54.

Given the well-known secretiveness of faery-kind, and their dislike of being spied upon, it is little surprise to read of the brownie of Stansted in Essex. This 'little man' worked in some stables, but when one of the stable boys deliberately concealed himself in the hayloft to have a look at the creature, he departed forever.[65]

Fortunately, not all brownies will depart precipitately and without warning. The spirit residing at Cullachy House in the Great Glen indicated his displeasure by moving all the furniture around at night- and then moving it back to its original place before dawn. Strangers in the house was particular cause of discontent.[66]

Food- 'Wages' & Offerings

As Robert Cromek described, the brownie will toil energetically and with scrupulous care, after which he will be "sweaty, dusty and fatigued" and will quite properly expect to be able to rest and restore himself. He will enter the kitchen and stir up the embers and will expect to find food awaiting him. This should be set out in an accessible place, but should never be described explicitly as either wages or a gift.
Reginald Scot described white bread and milk as the being's "standing fee," but this makes the interaction seem too contractual and formal. 'Reward,' 'recompense' or 'remuneration' are all terms too evocative of a commercial agreement. The brownie's expectation of food might be better

---

[64] C. Rogers, *Social Life in Scotland,* 1886, vol.3, 247; W. Henderson, *Notes on the Folklore of the Northern Counties,* 1879, 248; G. Henderson, *The Popular Rhymes, Sayings, and Proverbs of the County of Berwick,* 1865, 65-66; Westwood & Kingshill, *The Lore of Scotland,* 229; MacGregor, *Peat Fire Flame,* 55; Stoddard, *Remarks on the Local Scenery & Manners of Scotland During the Years 1799 & 1800,* 64.
[65] L. Newman, 'Notes on the Folklore of Cambridgeshire & the Eastern Counties,' *Folklore,* vol.56, 1945, 287-93.
[66] MacGregor, *Peat Fire Flame,* 53.

thought of as akin to the right or expectation of a family member to be fed. It is something that is done naturally and as a matter of course.[67]

The meat and drink must not be given directly: it must be 'left out'- available but not too obviously. It might be added that the brownie views the fire, as much as the food, as his right; hence, in one Scottish case when the servants stayed up too late, gossiping by the hearth, he appeared and told them "Gang awa' to your beds sirs, and dinna put out the wee grieshoch [embers]."[68]

The brownie's 'wages' were oatcakes made from meal warm from the mill, roughly shaped with knuckles, cooked on the fire's embers and spread with honey, curds or cream. Simple as the food may be, the brownie will eat to excess ("until he bursted" according to one account).[69] Modest as his tastes were, it was essential that there was no niggardliness. If a householder was parsimonious in the supply of food left out, their cooking, churning or cheesemaking would all be unsuccessful.[70]

One Scottish brownie, who helped his family by granting their wishes, was also fussy about his provisions. He was supplied with ham to eat, but one day he found the joint supplied too salty and, in his rage, stopped assisting the household, so that it lost everything. The reverse of this was the brownie of Bodsbeck who made do with the most meagre of rations and was deeply insulted when the master of the house left him more than that- albeit only bread and milk. The brownie of Strathmiglo Castle, in Fife, was said to be invisible. He didn't wait for food to be left out- instead he stole from the pantry,

[67] R. Cromek, *Remains of Nithsdale & Galloway Song,* 331; Scot, *Discoverie of Witchcraft,* 1584, Book 4, c.10.
[68] Scott, *Minstrelsy of the Scottish Borders,* 1802, vol.1, 53.
[69] W. Henderson, *Notes on the Folklore of the Northern Counties,* 1879, 248; Heron, *Observations Made on a Journey Through the Western Counties of Scotland,* 227.
[70] Sullivan, *Cumberland & Westmorland- Ancient & Modern,* 136.

which was the paid sign of his continued presence in the castle. [71]

Conscious and distinct offerings or sacrifices, as against the gifts that were pretended not to be such, were seen in the far north of Scotland. It's recorded that on Shetland every notable family was served by a "Browny or evil spirit" and in return for his service they would sprinkle a little milk at the corner of the house every time the churn was used and, when they brewed, some of the wort was poured into a hole on top of a so-called 'brownie's stone.' If such offerings were neglected, though, there would be retribution. In one case a man refused to offer any wort and preferred to read his bible instead: two brews failed because the brownie had been scorned. On the island of Inch, near Easdale in Argyll, the MacDougall's brownie was said to look after the cattle, but if he didn't get a share of their milk poured into his stone, a cow would fall over a cliff. By way of contrast, in 1808 in a description of the Shetland islands, one author took a more righteous view of the brownie as a kind of demon. If people refused to subjugate themselves any longer to his impious demands for 'sacrifice,' brews would fail; but if the brownie was ignored, he advised, the evil spirit would eventually desert the house and the brewing would come good again.[72]

Clothing & Laying

Ill-judged gifts of clothes or headgear are especially likely to 'lay' or drive a brownie away for, as one eighteenth century source stated: "brownies "seek nae claes."[73]

---

[71] *Tobar an dulchais,* Feb.16th 1979; Chambers, *Popular Rhymes,* 325.
[72] M. Martin, *A Description of the Western Isle of Scotland,* 1716, 391; J. Brand, *Description of Zetland,* 1808, 169; A. MacGregor, *Peat Fire Flame,* 47 & 56; S. Hibbert, *A Description of the Shetland Isles,*1891, 206; see too Cromek, *Remains of Nithsdale & Galloway Song,* 332.
[73] MacRitchie, *Testimony of Tradition,* 160.

Although they will pass most of their lives without ever uttering a word to the humans they serve, individual brownies will very regularly to express their displeasure with garments using verse. The broonie of Glendevon exclaimed:

> "Gie brownie coat, gie brownie sark,
> Ye'se get nae mair o' brownies wark."[74]

In this case, whilst there was a fundamental objection to being given clothes at all, an additional part of the problem appears to have been the manner in which the gift was offered. Had the clothes merely been laid out, they might have been accepted, but the farmer's wife brazenly called the brownie's attention to them, which formed (or compounded) the insulting nature of her indiscretion. In another instance, the brownie of one Shetland mill was seen to be a naked young man. He provided the miller with valuable assistance, feeding the grain into the upper millstones, but as soon as a person took pity on him and he was given some clothes, he abandoned the place in umbrage at the ill-conceived gesture.[75]

The foregoing notwithstanding, receipt of clothes is not automatically anathema to the brownie. Readers may recall Brownie Clod, who made an agreement to perform two men's work in return for a coat and cowl; he plainly chose to accept this remuneration and was happy with it in terms of both quantity and quality. Then again, at Dolphinton, in Roxburghshire, it was the *wrong* clothes that caused the offence:

> "Sin' ye gie me a harden ramp
> Nae mair o' your corn I will tramp."

---

[74] R. Chambers, *Popular Rhymes,* 3rd edition, 1870, 325- examples are given also from Bodsbeck, Claypots Castle, Dundee; Cromek, *Remains of Nithsdale & Galloway Song,* 332-333.
[75] Westwood & Kingshill, *The Lore of Scotland,* 79; Stewart, *Shetland Fireside Tales,* 134.

As we see in this last case, it might be the fabric ('harden'- a coarse hemp shirt) that was the problem- and this was a mistake often made. Reginald Scot recorded an identical complaint in 1584 ("Hemton, hamten- here I will never more tread or stampen") whilst one Lincolnshire brownie was clear about what he would have preferred to the rough material:

> "Harden, harden, harden hamp!
> I will neither grind nor stamp.
> Had you given me linen gear,
> I had served you many a year…"[76]

Alternatively, it might be that the items offered are old and worn or- conversely and contrarily- because they are brand new and specially made. So, the 'Little One' of the MacKays in Kintyre was seen to have injured himself on frozen ground, for he was leaving bloody footprints in the snow. The family wanted to give him shoes to protect his feet, but the laird's wife made the error of giving cast-offs that the children had grown out of. The brownie duly left. When King Broonie on Shetland was given a new cloak and hood (or hat) he abandoned the farm in question; so too, the gift of a new hat drove off Dobbs in Sussex.[77]

In some cases, it is the want of recompense that irks. One brownie at Glenmoriston in the Great Glen did a huge amount of threshing at night but felt exploited: he appeared before the farmer and warned him clearly what was required: "If brownie won't be getting bread or a hood/ Brownie will not be working anymore."[78]

---

[76] *New Statistical Account,* vol.3, 1845, 260- Oxnam; Westwood & Kingshill, *The Lore of Scotland,* 180; Scot, *Discoverie of Witchcraft,* 1584, Book 4, c.10; P. Binnall, 'A Brownie Legend from Lincolnshire,' *Folklore,* vol.51, 1940, 219

[77] Heron, *Observations Made on a Journey Through the Western Counties of Scotland,* 227; MacGregor, *Peat Fire Flame,* 49; B. Edmonston, *The Home of a Naturalist,* 1888, 203; L. N. Candlin, 'Sussex Sprites & Goblins,' *Sussex County Magazine,* vol.17, no.4, 1943, 96; J. Simpson, *Folklore of Sussex,* 1973, 57.

At Overthwaite, near Beetham in Cumbria, a farm brownie appeared in about 1650. He was known as the 'Tawny Boy,' reflective of his brown complexion, and for six months or so contributed much valuable labour, being well treated in return. However, when he was presented with a new suit of clothes and- perhaps worse- given a haircut against his will, he left, repeating a typical rhyme to express his grievances.[79]

At Boghall Farm near Dollar in Fife, it was a blanket that upset the brownie. The brownie was a very hard worker and was content with little in return: he slept on straw in the barn and ate just sowans (fermented oats) and sweet milk. However, one very cold winter the farmer's wife took pity on him and offered a warm covering for his bed. He cursed the blanket and departed, taking all the farm's good fortune with him. Notably, in his parting lament, he generously wished "success to Bogha' although brownie's away," suggesting that the connection and commitment to the place could persist even in the face of perceived insults.[80]

Readers may be left in some doubt as to how a person should behave to avoid antagonising a brownie. There is clearly no single rule applicable to all members of the species. The best advice must be to pay close attention to the behaviour of the individual brownie. Such sensitivity demonstrates respect for the being and is a clear statement that their labours are not taken for granted. They may work without being invited to do so, but their commitment still needs to be acknowledged, albeit it with subtlety and tact.

Banishing the Brownie

---

[78] MacGregor, *Peat Fire Flame*, 53.
[79] W. Hutton, *Beetham Repository*, 1770, 171.
[80] Westwood & Kingshill, *The Lore of Scotland*, 56; *County Folklore*, vol.7, 'Clackmannanshire,' 317; at Glendevon in the same county, clothes repelled the broonie.

Another guaranteed way of getting rid of a brownie is to baptise it. As we've already seen, the resident sprit of Dalswinton in Dumfriesshire was devoted to 'his' family- and most especially to one of the daughters. He fetched the midwife to her confinement when the servant instructed to do so was too slow (and chastised the young man for his sloth) but the young woman's new husband thought it would be a good idea to christen him, so holy water was thrown in the brownie's face. Of course, he instantly disappeared for ever. Sir Walter Scott gave a version of this incident which he situated near Jedburgh; his conclusion was different, but no happier for the human household: the laird was grateful for the brownie's dutiful service and, being told that the creature had expressed a wish for a green coat, one was provided. He took the garment- but left anyway.[81]

At Galdenock Mill in Galloway, a broonie undertook chores in the mill at night. This was valuable to the miller, but the being also played pranks and got on the nerves of the man's wife. She and the broonie quarrelled as a result, and in the course of their row she insulted him. The brownie took revenge by holding her over the fire, and then by dipping her in the well, after which he abandoned the property and his work for a while. Eventually, he returned, but he was even more troublesome than before, so it was decided to lay him. The local minister duly came to sing hymns and recite psalms at the mill. Initially, the broonie just mocked and interrupted the priest, but eventually he agreed to leave- more because he was worn down by the pious singing than because the Christian faith had proved anathema.[82]

Although most authorities on the subject are sure that the 'free' and tireless labour of the brownie is an asset to any house or farm, opinion is not unanimous on this. One writer

[81] T. Browning, *Dumfries & Galloway Folk Tales,* 2016, 57; J. Maxwell Wood, *Witchcraft & Superstitious Record in the South Western District of Scotland,* 1911, 188; Scott, *Minstrelsy of the Scottish Borders,* vol.1, 54.
[82] R. Trotter, *Galloway Gossip,* 1901, 46, 'The Haunted Mill.'

suggested that the brownie's toil was not generally sought after by individuals (were that even possible) and that most people who found they had a brownie attached to their property would happily have exorcised him and released themselves from the bond. This statement might confuse the brownie's labours with the habit of Scottish faeries to overhear an idle wish for help with a task and then demand more and more work to do- or it may reveal an unspoken truth- that the value of the work done has to be balanced with the nuisance of the pranks. Samuel Johnson seemed to imply something along the same lines when, in 1774, he recorded that the Scots now were content to save what they had given the brownies in 'wages' and to undertake themselves the jobs that he had previously performed.[83]

---

[83] 'A Sketch of Scottish Diablerie in General,' *Fraser's Magazine,* vol.25, 1842, 326; S. Johnson, *A Journey to the Western Isles of Scotland,* 1774, 'Ostig in Skye.'.

Related Beings

As stated at the beginning of the book, I have deliberately excluded various types of faery being- boggart, hobgoblin, lob and puck- which resemble brownies in various respects and yet are widely treated as being members of separate classes or species. There are, though, a number of creatures whose status is much more intermediate or uncertain.

Amongst those beings that have been viewed as relations of the brownie is the Killmoulis of the Border region. It lives in front of the fireplace in the grain drying kiln, guarding the mill and the miller. In addition, it has the gift of prophecy, being able to predict who a person will marry. This is discovered by throwing a length of thread into a pot and starting to rewind it into another ball. At some point, Killmoulis will grab the thread- if he is then asked "Who holds," he will name the future spouse (although it's also alleged that he has no mouth).[84]

Also in the Border counties of Scotland there lived a sprite called the Wag-at-t'-Wa that is often treated as a sort of brownie. It lived in the kitchen of farms, overseeing the work of the domestic servants but not actually undertaking any chores, unlike a brownie. Whenever the iron pot hook over the fire was free, the wag would swing there; he looked like an old man dressed in grey, except that he had long, crooked legs and a long tail, which helped him hang from the bracket. The wag approved of children, happiness in a household and lots of home-brewed ale. He would disappear if there was a death in a family and a cross marked on the pot crook would seemingly lay him- as he could no longer bear to touch it- although pushing the pot hook back and forth is believed to be a way of encouraging the Wag to return again.[85]

---

[84] W. Henderson, *Notes on the Folklore of the Northern Counties,* 1879, 252.
[85] Henderson, *Folklore of the Northern Counties,* 218-220.

We saw earlier the Herefordshire tradition of the 'brownie sway' over the fire; the Wag suggests it may once have been a more widespread phenomenon. Two conclusions are certain, though. The first is that- for all that's been said about the brownie's work ethic- they could be just as attached to their rest beside (or above) the fire. Secondly, it's notable that the iron bracket itself caused no problems. Many readers will be aware of the faery aversion to ferrous metals but, in this case, it was the addition of a cross that repelled the Wag, not the iron itself. What's more, much of the brownies' work will have involved handling iron and steel implements- scythes, reaping hooks and more- all of which was done voluntarily and without complaint. It therefore looks as though iron is a problem to faeries only if they come into contact with it against their wills.

Looking further north into central Scotland, the folklorist Alasdair Alpin MacGregor stated that every *clachan* (hamlet) or farm in Perthshire used to have its own brownie. These were associated with barns, where at night they would help to trash grain and sheave the corn stalks. They were wise and elderly looking and, as a result, were called the 'little old man of the barn.' The being is said to be over two hundred years old, but still very active. This *bodachan sabhaill* (as he's known in Gaelic) seems to be a sort of brownie, or very closely related.[86]

Even further north, at Baugh on the island of Tiree, a supernatural being used to herd the crofter's beasts at night, keeping them away from the crops. Although the mysterious herder was normally invisible, a man with the second sight saw him once as an almost naked creature. As a result, the helpful being was given shoes and breeches, in response to which the figure declared:

---

[86] MacGregor, *Peat Fire Flame,* 45; D. MacKenzie, *Wonder Tales from Scottish Myths,* 1917, c.14.

"Shoes and breeks on Gunna,
And Gunna at the herding,
But may Gunna enjoy neither shoes or breeks,
If he should herd the cattle anymore."

The kindly-meant gift therefore lost the locals their night-time guardian of the cattle. This very much indicates that 'Gunna' was a kind of brownie, albeit attached to a settlement rather than to any specific house or small holding. Rather than the name denoting to a type of being, it's been suggested that it is a personal name, derived from the Norse 'Gunnar,' although as far as we know, such an individual appellation would be unusual for a brownie. Of course, the truth may be that most brownies have just been better at concealing their real names from humans than the Gunna- something that many faeries prefer to do in order to preserve their privacy and power.[87]

In East Yorkshire another being of indeterminate classification is known. Robin Round-cap, as he's called, was connected to Spaldington Hall (between Howden and Market Weighton), where he laboured happily with his flail in the barn, but also played "elfish tricks" such as mixing the winnowed wheat grains back in with the chaff, putting out fires and knocking over milk pails. The prayers of three clergymen laid him in a well, which has borne his name since.[88]

Robin is also known from Holderness, in East Yorkshire, where he has been classified as a hob thrust. He will do housemaids' work but, if he's annoyed, he will break crockery, rattle pans, spill the milk pails and let beer run to waste from the vats. In one case, he'd made life so miserable that the family he was attached to tried to escape him. This attempt to leave the nuisance being behind led to a typical 'faery flitting'

[87] MacGregor, *Peat Fire Flame,* 46; Westwood & Kingshill, *The Lore of Scotland,* 459-460; on the issue of faery names, see my *British Fairies,* Green Magic, 2017, c.19 and *Who's Who in Faerieland,* Green Magic, 2022, c.2.
[88] *County Folklore,* vol.6, 'East Yorkshire,' 54;

story, in that it met with failure, as the family realised that Robin was coming with them to their new home, making all the effort pointless. The resolution of laying in a well is assigned to this case as well. In this connection, it may be significant that a pamphlet of 1692 made reference to Dobse's (that is, Dob's) Well near to Oundle. This may also be a site to which a dobbie was exorcised, unless in this case the being had a healing function like some other faeries in wells.[89]

Similar household goblins of uncertain pedigree are known elsewhere. There was in Lincolnshire, at Goxhill, near to East Halton, which was said to resemble the broonie and Robin Round-cap and others in the North Riding of Yorkshire, where they were termed 'hobmen' but likened to the Scottish brownie. One lived at Hob Hill, Upleatham, and served on a farm owned by the Oughtred family, performing all the usual chores of turning the hay, bringing the cattle to and from pastures, winnowing grain and topping and tailing turnips. He was active until about 1820, when a labourer's coat left hanging on a winnowing machine was mistaken by him as an unwanted gift and led to his departure. It's not apparent if the term 'hobman' that was applied here might have implied any subtle distinction between a hobgoblin or hobthrush and other beings, such as brownies. They were perhaps considered to be a little more human in their characteristics- possibly being like those brownies who were described as resembling young or old men.[90]

Finally, whilst we have heard much about brownies being driven away by poor treatment, we very seldom discover where they go to. We know that the Bodsbeck brownie transferred his allegiance to Liethin Hall (or vice versa) but for the rest we have to assume that they retreated to their hiding

---

[89] J. Nicholson, *Folklore of East York*shire, 1890, 80-81; Scott, 'The Devil & His Imps,' *Transactions of the American Philological Association*, vol. 26, 88; on wells, see my *Faeries & the Natural World,* Green Magic, 2021, c.4.
[90] *County Folklore,* vol.5, 'Lincolnshire,' 56; Blakeborough, *Wit, Character, Folklore and Customs of the North Riding of Yorkshire,* 204.

places in hollow trees and the like and brooded there. This makes me wonder whether certain malevolent beings of the Scottish Borders might best be considered as disgruntled former brownies.

The *powrie* or *dunter* haunts the old fortified houses called pele towers and makes a noise like the pounding of flax or grain. When this is louder than usual, or goes on for longer than was normal, it is a sure sign of an impending death or misfortune. The Redcap of the same region is a malevolent, goblin-like being said to lurk in ruined towers and castles and to dye his headwear in the blood of the victims he kills with his spear. He is a "short, thick-set old man, with long prominent teeth [and] grisly hair streaming down to his shoulders…" This description is very similar to several of brownies that we have seen. What's more, we've noted already that some brownies choose to remain in the former castles of their human family, even after the permanent home has moved elsewhere, and that some have the power of foretelling death. Perhaps the noises made by the Powrie might be some echo of the useful toil he used to engage in before becoming disaffected. All that can be said is that the Powrie, dunter and redcap all share characteristics of the broonie and live in close proximity to him, indicating that a link is not impossible.[91]

---

[91] W. Henderson, *Notes on the Folklore of the Northern Counties,* 255-6 & 253-5; see too Westwood & Kingshill, *Lore of Scotland,* 126 & 246-247.

Brownies in British Culture

Although not the most numerous of faery types, the brownie has become quite a well-known figure of British art and literature. As mentioned much earlier, James Hogg fictionalised the *Brownie of Bodsbeck* in a short story of 1818 and William Nicholson wrote the poem *The Brownie of Blednoch.*[92] Both works fed back into folklore in a curious process of reinforcement, so that what was traditional and what had been derived from the literary compositions became confused. Arguably, this very book perpetuates that tendency, by using some of Hogg and Nicholson's descriptions of the brownies as evidence.[93]

Other writers have used and elaborated upon traditional materials in successful works. In 1874 Juliana Horatia Ewing composed *Lob Lie by the Fire, or the Luck of Lingborough,* which adapted the 'lubber fiend' or hob best known from Milton's *L'Allegro* (1631) and thereby created an authentic-feeling story that presents itself as the retelling of an old folk tale from the north of England. Lob brings luck to the old hall through his thorough and untiring work and the residents respect him: they don't speak about their good fortune and they don't spy on him when he is toiling as they know "that the Good People don't like to be watched at work." Because Lob was present, the farm's productivity thrived and thieves and predators did no harm.

In 1955, faery-lore expert Katherine Briggs tried her hand at the same thing, with her wistful children's story of *Hobberdy Dick*, which is set in the Cotswolds during the Civil war. As is to be expected from this author, the story is full of authentic folklore detail, but it is also a surprisingly rich and melancholy tale- a minor treasure of the genre.

---

[92] For Nicholson's poem see the Appendix.
[93] Henderson & Cowan, *Scottish Fairy Belief,* 26 & 201.

The word brownie became even more familiar in popular culture when it was decided to give this name to the junior girl guides in 1914. The name was taken from another story by Juliana Ewing, in which two children learn that in life they can be either helpful brownies or lazy boggarts. Originally Baden-Powell had chosen the name of 'Rosebuds' for the little girls' troop, so perhaps it was wisely replaced; nonetheless, the substitute label was inappropriate for other reasons. As we know, female brownies are actually rare, and the few we know of seem to be as hairy, muscular and potentially dangerous as their male counter-parts. Baden-Powell had in mind a very different conception of the brownie function: the movement was meant to socialise girls into their roles as carers and providers, little 'elves' doing the housework for their mothers as preparation for serving and supporting their later husbands.

Juliana Ewing was born in Yorkshire in 1841, and whilst she was growing up she often acted as storyteller to the rest of her family- performing something of a 'brownie' role in aid of her mother. When she was 23, her best-known story, *The Brownies*, was published in the *Monthly Packet* magazine with illustrations by George Cruikshank. Both *The Brownies* and the related *Lob-lie-by-the-fire* ostensibly concern household elves, and relay much traditional lore about them, but in fact both stories are moralising tales that demythologise their subjects, rationalising faery phenomena and seeking everyday explanations for incidents- as was so common amongst folklore collectors of the period. As a result, *Lob Lie by the Fire* is revealed to be just the orphaned stable boy John Brown, whilst in *The Brownies* we are let in on the secret well before the end that "All children are Brownies" and that "there [are] no brownies but children." In fact, although Mrs Ewing knew her folklore very well, she was far more interested in teaching children to be helpful and obedient to their parents than she was in recording authentic accounts and themes. In fact, folk tradition was distorted to fit her 'improving' messages.

This can be seen very clearly in the plot of *The Brownies*. Two lazy and selfish boys called Tommy and Johnnie are taught the virtues of helping their widowed father with his trade and household chores:

> "The Brownies, or, as they are sometimes called, the Small Folk, the Little People, or the Good People, are a race of tiny beings who domesticate themselves in a house of which some grown-up human being pays the rent and taxes... When they are idle and mischievous, they are called Boggarts, and are a curse to the house they live in. When they are useful and considerate, they are Brownies, and are a much-coveted blessing... in time these Little People are Brownies no longer. They grow up into men and women."

When Tommy and Johnnie have learned their lesson and begin to help their father, good luck returns to the house:

> "Before long Tommy began to work for the farmers, and Baby grew up into a Brownie, and made (as girls are apt to make) the best house-sprite of all. For, in the Brownie's habits of self-denial, thoughtfulness, consideration, and the art of little kindnesses, boys are, I am afraid, as a general rule, somewhat behindhand with their sisters… For these Brownies -young ladies!- are much desired as wives, whereas a man might as well marry an old witch as a young Boggartess."

The next significant appearance of brownies was in the work of Canadian illustrator Palmer Cox (1840-1924). He produced a series of brownie titles which have been claimed as "the first commercial comic books." Each of these dozen books were prefaced by a brief statement that:

> "Brownies, like fairies and goblins, are imaginary little sprites, who are supposed to delight in harmless pranks and helpful deeds. They work and sport while weary

households sleep, and never allow themselves to be seen by mortal eyes."

This is a fair summary of the established lore, but it is not reflected in the books themselves, which comprise numerous illustrations interspersed amongst verse- for example, here is the 'Brownies' ride' from *The Brownies: Their Book* of 1887:

"One night a cunning Brownie band
Was roaming through a farmer's land
And while the rogues went prying round,
The farmer's mare at rest they found."

A small selection of the series titles and chapter headings will illustrate how far Cox had travelled from authenticity. In his first book, *The Brownies*, readers were entertained by brownies on skates, bicycles and roller skates, brownies playing tennis and baseball and brownies enjoying canoeing and tobogganing and visiting a gym, the seaside and a toy shop. In 1890's *Another Brownie Book* readers were amused by brownies fishing, kite flying, yacht racing, learning to swim and dance and attending a fancy ball. And so on- the books were immensely popular and were used in their marketing by some forty companies including Kodak (the 'box brownie' camera) and Proctor and Gamble.

In Palmer's *The Brownies and Prince Florimel* brownies are described as being the size of twelve-year-olds, often perching on fences and hiding adroitly whenever danger threatens. This conforms to conventional faery imagery, but as will have been seen in the verse quoted earlier, Cox had them partaking of their adventures in swarms, more like pixies or spriggans than the solitary creatures they were originally conceived as. In the same story, by the way, the faeries are ruled by Queen Titania and are tiny; they "never grew old and always remained beautiful. Their loveliness of face and form was beyond all description. Just try to think of the prettiest girl you ever saw. Well, even the plainest of these fairies were ever so much prettier."

In the 1920s and '30s Enid Blyton adopted brownies as the subjects of several children's books, including *The Book of the Brownies, The Little Brownie House, Snicker the Brownie, The Brownie Who Pulled Faces, My First Nature Book- Brownie Magic* and several others. The first book mentioned seems typical of Blyton's output: naughty brownies Hop, Skip and Jump are always playing tricks; they are then tricked themselves by Witch Green Eyes into helping her to abduct fairy princess Peronel. For this the three are expelled from faeryland and set out on an adventure to rescue the princess. Very much like Cox, Blyton's brownies seem a good deal more like pixies than the traditional solitary creatures who labour on farms.

It was not until the late 1990s and the appearance of the Harry Potter series that brownies were restored in children's literature to something more closely resembling their original folklore character. J K Rowling had plainly studied folk traditions- and the history of alchemy and magic- quite extensively before writing her books; this is demonstrated by her treatment of Dobby and the other house-elves, and not least in the traditional name she chose for her main brownie character.

In the series, house-elves are depicted as magical creatures who are intensely devoted and loyal to those designated as their masters. House-elves serve wizards and witches, usually being found in the employment of old wizarding families, and they are bound to do everything that their masters command- unless they are freed. A house-elf can only be freed when their master presents them with clothes (as we know, a classic element in brownie lore). In part due to their absolute obedience, house-elves are treated very brutally by their owners: they have no rights of their own and are viewed as slaves, without feeling or emotions. To symbolise this, they usually wear makeshift clothes made from found objects such as pillowcases and rags (again, typical of the traditional brownie). These garments can become quite filthy, yet- as a further expression of the fact that they have no needs other than those specifically allowed to them by their masters- the house-elf will not clean them. Indeed, so subservient are they that house-elves will torture and maim themselves if they think they have displeased their master. Large numbers of house-elves are also employed at Hogwarts School of Witchcraft and Wizardry. They work the kitchens, preparing feasts for the entire school. They also move luggage to and from rooms and clean the dormitories and other areas.

The Society for the Promotion of Elfish Welfare (S.P.E.W.) was group founded by Hogwarts student Hermione Granger in response to what she saw as gross injustice in the treatment of house elves during the quidditch world cup. Despite attracting little interest or sympathy in her campaign from fellow students, Hermione persisted, employing tactics such as badge-making and petitioning, albeit with very little effect. Eventually, she started knitting hats and socks which she left lying around, hoping to free some unsuspecting elf who picked them up and put them on while cleaning the common room. In due course, the elves became angry at Hermione's attempts at liberation by stealth. The friendliest house-elves working at the school, Dobby and Winky, were considered disgraces by the rest of their colleagues; this was due to Dobby accepting payment and a holiday. Winky, meanwhile, feel into despair after she lost her master, turning to drink and doing no work.

Rowling's are serious and rounded characters. She preserves the significance of clothes to their release and incorporates the brownies' work ethic, although the element of enslavement against which Hermione campaigns is not derived from British tradition.

Modern Brownies

Earlier I discussed the story of Meg Mullach in Strathspey. This being was first recorded by John Aubrey in his *Hermetick Philosophy*, published in 1696. Interestingly, even then, he referred to Meg and her brother, Brownie Clod, as haunting the Grant family "of old." As the writer William Forsyth later observed, this phraseology was "very significant: Meg Mollach and Brownie were still hidden in the dim and distant past two hundred years ago."[94]

Many commentators, from the early eighteenth century onwards, were insistent that belief in the brownie was fading. In 1716 Martin Martin wrote his *Description of the Western Isles of Scotland,* in which he noted that "not long since," it had been the habit of the islanders to make offerings of milk and wort to the "spirit they called browny." Even in one of our earliest accounts of the brownie's character, therefore, there is a suggestion that he was already a thing of the past. Thomas Pennant, describing the Hebrides in 1772, said the brownie was "now put to flight;" Samuel Johnson declared that on Skye "nothing has been heard [of him] for many years" whilst in the same year on Shetland George Low pronounced the brownies to be "losing ground." Twenty-five years later, Sir John Stoddard again reported the brownie to have been believed in "until recently." In 1808 John Brand, in his *Description of Zetland* (Shetland), advised his readers that "Not above forty to fifty years ago every family had an evil spirit called a Browny, which served them and to whom they sacrificed." This is a highly tendentious summary of the tradition, but (once again) it pins the loss of belief down to the previous generation.[95]

---

[94] Forsyth, *In the Shadow of Cairngorm,* 1900, c.4.
[95] Martin, *Description,* 391; Pennant, *A Tour in Scotland,* 359; Johnson, *A Journey to the Western Isles,* 1774; Low, *A Tour Through the Islands,* 1774, 82; Stoddard, *Remarks on Local Scenery,* 1800, 64; J. Brand, *Description of Zetland,* 1808, 169.

Lastly, Robert Heron summarised the general view when he declared that in 1793, "tales of Ghosts, Brownies, Fairies and Witches are the frequent entertainment of a winter's evening amongst the native peasantry of Kirkcudbright" but that, by that date, the brownie was "seldom heard of." All in all, the picture painted was clear: from quite an early date the brownie had fallen out of popular credence and was now just an amusing story- even for simple and credulous folk.[96]

What had driven the brownie away so early- apparently even before other faery beings? John Dalyell reported that it was the Reformation that had "chained" the brownie, with credulity in such imaginary beings abating in the late seventeenth century. George Stewart said much the same of Shetland: the Gospel had driven the brownies, the trows and the tangie away and all had sought sanctuary on the Faroes. As we saw earlier, Robert Hunt in his *Popular Romances of the West of England* (1865) ascribed the disappearance of the 'Browney' from Cornwall to national schooling rather than to the Protestant religion.[97]

These opinions naturally rely upon the ideas that there is a necessary antipathy between education and superstition and, even more acutely, between faery-kind and Christianity. This is an idea which primarily derives in turn from the belief that faeries are a remnant of the fallen angels who followed Lucifer in his rebellion in heaven, but never quite got to hell, being trapped instead on earth. This is, of course, just one theory of faery origins, one that has been shaped by a powerful need to accommodate them within the parameters of biblical text. In addition, as I have described elsewhere, much that was written about the disappearance of the brownie is merely a specific example of a wider tendency to regard faery beings as 'only just' vanished, a belief of one's grandparents' generation that has relatively recently fallen from fashion. As such, the

---

[96] Heron, *Observations Made in a Journey,* 1793, 227.
[97] J. Dalyell, *Darker Superstitions of Scotland,* 1835, 530; Stewart, *Shetland Fireside Tales,* 134.

date for the loss of belief is always a few decades before any particular writer records their comments. Witness the words of famed folklorist Andrew Lang, writing in reference to the Borders in 1913:

> "Belief in the Brownie died hard in the Border; I am not sure that, in remote 'up the water' districts, he did not survive almost till the advent of motor cars and bicycles."

Here, technology- rather than the New Testament- has driven the faery away, but the key point is, again, that it has *only recently* happened.[98]

Predictably, in fact, the brownies have not vanished. In late June 1923 Geoffrey Hodson reported that he had seem some beings that he called brownies in a wood on the Lake District. He said he had discovered a colony of them near Thirlmere; they were six inches high and lived in tiny thatched cottages. They wore brown suits with pointed hats and boots and were bearded. In November 1926 Hodson saw more on Helvellyn, very similar to the others except that they were dressed in green.

These beings were untypical of brownies for their woodland abode, but in January 1922 Hodson also saw a brownie in a house in Preston, dressed in green with a brown conical hat. This being was "lively and familiar" he reported. Overall, he stated that the brownies he encountered worked as smiths or miners, lived in tribes and were friendly and communicative. He also encountered beings he classed as 'brownies' in June 1925 near to Geneva, seeing large numbers of figures about one foot six inches tall who were carrying tools and talking in guttural tones to each other. In August the same year, in the Cotswolds, he sighted more brownies about one foot tall; their brown suits and caps were traditional brownie clothing, he averred. They were walking or dancing whilst communicating,

---

[98] A. Lang, *Highways & Byways in the Border,* 1913, 31; see my *Faery- A Guide to the Lore, Magic & World of the Good Folk,* 2020, c.14.

albeit without audible words. Despite the regularity and richness of his experiences, then, in almost every detail Hodson's brownies departed from the character and appearance known to British tradition. If I were to choose a better label for whatever he saw, I would opt for Paracelsus' 'gnomes.'[99]

In Marjorie Johnson's Seeing Fairies (2014), there are no mentions of brownies. This does not, though, mean that they were absent from mid-twentieth century Britain and that witnesses did not see them. Quite a few of the reports collected by Johnson describe seeing 'gnomes' in houses, or working in gardens with spades and rakes. I suspect these were sightings of what earlier generations would have instinctively called brownies; Paracelsus' neologism 'gnome' comes more naturally to us now, whereas the older label does not seem so familiar- but what is described is identical.[100]

It is encouraging to discover that brownies are still being encountered today- and not just in Britain, but across the world. In the Fairy Census (2014-17) several people reported sightings of brownie-like beings, as well as using the term to try to classify and describe other supernaturals they had seen. A man in Cambridgeshire in the 2010s glimpsed a small brownie or gnome inside his house late one evening. A woman living in Aberdeenshire stated that she was familiar with a brownie called Snodgrass, who always carried a broom, whilst during the same period in Rhondda, another middle-aged woman reported a brownie sharing the house with her family.[101]

Despite entering a new millennium, therefore, the key elements of the traditional British brownie persist- his connection with the home and his commitment to work. We

---

[99] Hodson, Fairies at Work & Play, c.1; The Kingdom of Faerie, c.6.
[100] M. Johnson, Seeing Fairies, 20, 21, 36, 100, 157, 158 & 172.
[101] Fairy Census, nos 12, 164B & 190; brownies were used as terms of reference in cases 75, 197, 370 & 389C (including USA & Canada).

have also come to accept that awareness of supernatural entities can exist alongside modern technology and lifestyles and that it is no longer embarrassing and uneducated to confess to witnessing such phenomena.

Appendix

William Nicholson (1782–1849) was a Scottish poet, who was born in the village of Borgue in Kirkcudbrightshire. He was encouraged in his writing by another dialect poet, James Hogg and came to be known as The Bard of Galloway, the 'pedlar-poet' and, simply, 'Wandering Wull.' In his work he made use of his native Scots speech and intended many of his lyrics to be sung. Nicholson's published collections include *Tales, in Verse*, and *Miscellaneous Poems: Descriptive of Rural Life and Manners* which the poem 'The Fairy Dance.' He is probably best remembered for 'The Brownie of Blednoch' (1828). The poem nicely summarises the alarming appearance of the brownie, his dwelling places, the huge range of tasks he undertook, and the modest recompense he asked for- all of which are lost to the community through the gift of some breeches.

The Brownie Of Blednoch

There cam a strange wight to our town-en'
And the fient a body did him ken';[102]
He tirled na lang, but he glided ben[103]
Wi' a dreary, dreary hum.

His face did glare like the glow o' the west,
When the drumlie cloud has it half o'ercast;[104]
Or the struggling moon when she's sair distrest--
O sirs! 'twas Aiken-drum.

I trow the bauldest stood aback,
Wi' a gape and a glower till their lugs did crack,[105]
As the shapeless phantom mum'ling spak-
"Hae ye wark for Aiken-drum?"

---

[102] *The fient a-* nobody at all.
[103] *Tirled-* spun; *ben-* inside.
[104] *Drumlie-* gloomy.
[105] *Lugs-* ears.

O had ye seen the bairns' fright,
As they stared at this wild and unyirthly wight,[106]
As he stauket in 'tween the dark and the light,[107]
And graned out, "Aiken-drum!"

"Sauf us!" quoth Jock, "d'ye see sic een;"[108]
Cries Kate, "There's a hole where a nose should hae been;
And the mouth's like a gash which a horn had ri'en;[109]
Wow! keep's frae Aiken-drum!"

The black dog, growling, cowered his tail,
The lassie swarfed, loot fa' the pail,[110]
Rob's lingle brack as he men't the flail, [111]
At the sight o' Aiken-drum.

His matted head on his breast did rest,
A lang blue beard wan'ered down like a vest;
But the glare o' his e'e nae Bard hath exprest,
Nor the skimes o' Aiken-drum.[112]

Roun' his hairy form there was naething seen
But a philibeg o' the rashes green,[113]
And his knotted knees played ay knoit between;
What a sight was Aiken-drum!

On his wauchie arms three claws did meet,[114]
As they trailed on the grun' by his taeless feet;
E'en the auld guidman himsel' did sweat,

---

[106] *Unyirthly*- unearthly
[107] *Stauket*- prowled.
[108] *Sic een*- such eyes.
[109] *Ri'en*- riven.
[110] *Swarfed*- swooned; *loot fa'*- let fall.
[111] *Lingle brack*- the strap holding the halves of his flail broke.
[112] *Skimes*- glances.
[113] *Philibeg*- a plaid.
[114] *Wauchie*- weak.

To look at Aiken-drum.

But he drew a score, himsel' did sain,[115]
The auld wife tried, but her tongue was gane;
While the young ane closer clasped her wean,
And turned frae Aiken-drum.

But the canny auld wife cam' till her breath,
And she deemed the Bible might ward aff scaith,[116]
Be it benshee, bogle, ghaist, or wraith-
But it fear'dna Aiken-drum.

"His presence protect us!" quoth the auld guidman;
"What wad ye, whare won ye- by sea or by lan'?
I conjure ye speak- by the Beuk in my haun!"[117]
What a grane gae Aiken-drum.

"I lived in a lan' whar we saw nae sky,
I dwalt in a spot whare a burn rins na by;
But I'se dwall now wi' you, if ye like to try-
Hae ye wark for Aiken-drum?

"I'll shiel' a' your sheep i' the mornin' sune,[118]
I'll berry your crap by the light o' the moon,[119]
And baa the bairns wi' an unken'd tune,[120]
If ye'll keep puir Aiken-drum.

"I'll loup the linn when ye canna wade,[121]
I'll kirn the kirn, and I'll turn the bread;[122]
And the wildest fillie that ever ran rede
I'se tame't," quoth Aiken-drum!

---

[115] Sain- *bless.*
[116] *Scaith*- harm.
[117] *Beuk in my haun*- the book in my hand (i.e. the Bible).
[118] *Shiel'*- to herd stock on a summer pasture.
[119] *Berry your crap*- thresh your grain.
[120] *Baa*- to lull or soothe.
[121] *Loup the linn*- jump over the waterfall, or rapids.
[122] *Kirn the kirn*- churn butter in the milk-churn.

"To wear the tod frae the flock on the fell-[123]
To gather the dew frae the heather-bell-
And to look at my face in your clear crystal well,
Might gie pleasure to Aiken-drum.

"I'se seek nae guids, gear, bond, nor mark;
I use nae beddin', shoon, nor sark;
But a cogfu' o' brose 'tween the light and dark,[124]
Is the wage o' Aiken-drum."

Quoth the wylie auld wife, "The thing speaks weel;
Our workers are scant- we hae routh o' meal;[125]
Gif he'll do as he says- be he man, be he de'il,
Wow! we'll try this Aiken-drum."

But the wenches skirled "He's no' be here!
His eldritch look gars us swarf wi' fear,
And the fient a ane will the house come near,
If they think but o' Aiken-drum.

"For a foul and a stalwart ghaist is he,
Despair sits brooding aboon his e'e bree,
And unchancie to light o' a maiden's e'e,
Is the grim glower o' Aiken-drum."

"Puir slipmalabors! ye hae little wit;[126]
Is'tna Hallowmas now, and the crap out yet?"
Sae she silenced them a' wi' a stamp o' her fit;
"Sit yer wa's down, Aiken-drum."

Roun' a' that side what wark was dune,
By the streamer's gleam, or the glance o' the moon;
A word or a wish- and the Brownie cam' sune,

---

[123] *Tod*- fox: to scare the fox away from the flocks.
[124] *Cogfu'*- a small cupful of gruel.
[125] *Routh*- plenty.
[126] *Slip-me-labours*- an untrustworthy or lazy person.

Sae helpfu' was Aiken-drum.

But he slade ay awa' or the sun was up,
He ne'er could look straught on Macmillan's cup;
They watched- but nane saw him his brose ever sup,
Nor a spune sought Aiken-drum.

On Blednoch banks, and on crystal Cree,
For mony a day a toiled wight was he;
While the bairns played harmless roun' his knee,
Sae social was Aiken-drum.

But a new-made wife, fu' o' rippish freaks,[127]
 Fond o' a things feat for the first five weeks,
 Laid a mouldy pair o' her ain man's breeks;
By the brose o' Aiken-drum.

Let the learned decide, when they convene,
What spell was him and the breeks between;
For frae that day forth he was nae mair seen,
And sair missed was Aiken-drum.

He was heard by a herd gaun by the Thrieve,
Crying "Lang, lang now may I greet and grieve;
For alas! I hae gotten baith fee and leave,
O, luckless Aiken-drum."

Awa'! ye wrangling sceptic tribe,
Wi' your pros and your cons wad ye decide
'Gain the 'sponsible voice o' a hale country-side
On the facts 'bout Aiken-drum?

Though the 'Brownie o' Blednoch' lang be gane,
The mark o' his feet's left on mony a stane;
 And mony a wife and mony a wean
Tell the feats o' Aiken-drum.

---

[127] *Rippish-* capricious or whimsical.

E'en now, light loons that jibe and sneer
At spiritual guests and a' sic gear,
At the Glashnoch Mill hae swat wi' fear,
 And looked roun' for Aiken-drum.

And guidly fo'ks hae gotten a fright,
When the moon was set, and the stars gied nae light,
At the roaring linn in the howe o' the night,
Wi' sughs like Aiken-drum.[128]

---

[128] *Sughs*- Sighs or heavy breathing.

Printed in Great Britain
by Amazon

40618879R00036